THE BASIC GUIDE TO CRYPTO TRADING

ALEXANDER FOSTER

"Push past personal limitations, and achieve
amazing things"

ALEXANDER FOSTER

CONTENTS

CHAPTER 1:
INTRODUCTION TO
CRYPTOCURRENCY TRADING

What is cryptocurrency and why is it valuable?

- Cryptocurrency is a decentralised digital currency that uses cryptography to secure transactions and control the creation of new units.

- Cryptocurrency is valuable because it offers several advantages over traditional forms of currency, including privacy, security, and decentralisation.

Understanding the blockchain technology:

- Blockchain is the underlying technology behind cryptocurrencies, which allows for secure and transparent record-keeping.

- Blockchain is a distributed ledger that is maintained by a network of computers, which allows for transactions to be validated and recorded without the need for intermediaries.

Risks and opportunities of cryptocurrency trading:

- There are several risks involved in cryptocurrency trading, including volatility, regulation, and security.

- However, there are also many opportunities in cryptocurrency trading, including potential for high returns, global accessibility, and technological innovation.

By understanding the risks and opportunities of cryptocurrency trading, you can make informed decisions about whether or not to invest in this exciting and rapidly evolving field.

.

CHAPTER 2:
GETTING STARTED WITH CRYPTO TRADING

Setting up a cryptocurrency exchange account:

- To get started with cryptocurrency trading, you'll need to set up an account with a reputable cryptocurrency exchange.

- This involves providing personal information and going through a verification process to ensure compliance with KYC (know your customer) and AML (anti-money laundering) regulations.

Depositing and withdrawing funds:

- Once your account is set up, you can deposit funds using various methods such as bank transfer, credit card, and cryptocurrency deposit.

- Understand the fees associated with each method and the processing times involved.

Withdrawing funds is a similar process, and it's important to understand the withdrawal fees and limits as well as the security measures involved in storing and transferring cryptocurrency.

- Withdrawing funds is a similar process, and it's important to understand the withdrawal fees and limits as well as the security measures involved in storing and transferring cryptocurrency.

Choosing the right cryptocurrencies to trade:

- Before you start trading, it's important to research and select the right cryptocurrencies to trade based on factors such as market cap, trading volume, and project fundamentals.

- Diversify your portfolio to minimise risk and maximise potential returns.

By understanding how to set up an exchange account, deposit and withdraw funds, and choose the right cryptocurrencies to trade, you can get started with cryptocurrency trading and begin to take advantage of the many opportunities in this exciting and rapidly evolving field.

CHAPTER 3:
TECHNICAL ANALYSIS FOR CRYPTO TRADING

Understanding candlestick charts and other technical indicators:

- Technical analysis is a popular approach to cryptocurrency trading that involves analysing price and volume data to identify patterns and make trading decisions.

- Candlestick charts are a common way to display this data, and it's important to understand how to read and interpret them.

- Other technical indicators, such as moving averages and relative strength index (RSI), can also be used to identify trends and predict price movements.

Identifying support and resistance levels:

- Support and resistance levels are key price levels that can help you make trading decisions.

- Support levels are price levels where buying pressure is strong enough to prevent the price from falling further, while resistance levels are price levels where selling pressure is strong enough to prevent the price from rising further.

By identifying these levels using technical analysis, you can set stop-loss and take-profit orders to manage your risk and maximise your potential returns.

CHAPTER 4:
FUNDAMENTAL ANALYSIS FOR CRYPTO TRADING

Understanding the factors that affect cryptocurrency prices:

- Fundamental analysis is another approach to cryptocurrency trading that involves analysing the underlying factors that drive cryptocurrency prices.

- Factors such as project fundamentals, adoption, and regulation can all have a significant impact on cryptocurrency prices.

- By understanding how these factors interact and affect each other, you can make informed trading decisions and position yourself for long-term success.

Following news and social media to stay up-to-date:

- Staying up-to-date with the latest news and developments in the cryptocurrency industry is important for making informed trading decisions.

- Social media and online communities can be a great source of information and insights into the latest trends and market sentiment.

- Following the right people and communities, you can stay ahead of the curve and position yourself for success in cryptocurrency trading.

Analysing market trends and investor sentiment:

- Market trends and investor sentiment are also important factors to consider when trading cryptocurrencies.

- Sentiment analysis tools can help you gauge market sentiment and make trading decisions based on the overall mood of the market.

- Order book analysis is another approach that can help you identify key price levels and potential trends based on the trading activity of other market participants.

By understanding how to use fundamental analysis and other tools to analyse market trends and investor sentiment, you can become a more effective cryptocurrency trader and take advantage of the many opportunities in this exciting and rapidly evolving field.

CHAPTER 5:
RISK MANAGEMENT IN CRYPTO TRADING

Setting stop-loss orders and take-profit orders:

- Setting stop-loss and take-profit orders is an important part of managing risk in cryptocurrency trading.

- Stop-loss orders can help you limit your losses if the price moves against you, while take-profit orders can help you lock in profits if the price moves in your favour.

- Set appropriate levels for these orders based on your trading strategy and risk tolerance.

Managing position size and leverage:

- Managing your position size and using leverage effectively are important for maximising profits while minimising risk.

- Position sizing involves determining the appropriate amount of capital to allocate to each trade based on your account balance and risk tolerance.

- Leverage can amplify your potential returns, but it can also increase your risk, so it's important to use it wisely and understand the potential consequences.

Diversifying your portfolio to minimise risk:

- Diversification is another important part of managing risk in cryptocurrency trading.

- By diversifying your portfolio across different cryptocurrencies and asset classes, you can reduce your exposure to any one particular market or asset.

- Consider the potential correlation between different assets and how they may perform in different market conditions.

By understanding how to set stop-loss and take-profit orders, manage position sizing and leverage, and diversify your portfolio, you can become a more effective cryptocurrency trader and minimise your risk while maximising your potential returns.

CHAPTER 6:
ADVANCED TRADING STRATEGIES

Day trading, swing trading, and long-term investing:

- There are different approaches to cryptocurrency trading, each with its own advantages and risks.

- Day trading involves buying and selling cryptocurrencies within a single day, while swing trading involves holding positions for a few days to a few weeks.

- Long-term investing involves holding positions for several months to several years.

By understanding the advantages and risks of each approach, you can choose the one that best suits your goals and risk tolerance.

Using margin and futures trading to maximise profits:

- Margin and futures trading are advanced trading strategies that can allow you to increase your potential profits.

- Margin trading allows you to borrow funds from the exchange to increase your position size, while futures trading allows you to speculate on the future price of a cryptocurrency.

- However, both strategies also increase your risk, so it's important to use them wisely and understand the potential consequences.

Trading altcoins and ICOs for higher risk/reward opportunities:

- Altcoins and ICOs (initial coin offerings) are higher risk/reward opportunities that can offer significant returns if you're willing to take on the extra risk.

- Altcoins are cryptocurrencies other than Bitcoin, while ICOs are a way for new cryptocurrency projects to raise funds by selling tokens to investors.

- Understand the risks and opportunities of trading altcoins and ICOs, you can make informed decisions and potentially maximise your returns.

By understanding how to use advanced trading strategies such as day trading, swing trading, and long-term investing, as well as margin and futures trading, and trading altcoins and ICOs, you can become a more effective cryptocurrency trader and potentially maximise your profits in this exciting and rapidly evolving field.

CHAPTER 7:
TIPS FOR SUCCESS IN CRYPTO TRADING

Developing a trading plan and sticking to it:

- Developing a trading plan is an important part of success in cryptocurrency trading.

- Your trading plan should include your goals, trading strategy, risk management plan, and rules for entering and exiting trades.

- By sticking to your plan and avoiding emotional trading decisions, you can increase your chances of success in cryptocurrency trading.

Controlling your emotions and avoiding FOMO and FUD:

- Emotions can be a major factor in cryptocurrency trading and can lead to impulsive and irrational trading decisions.

- FOMO (fear of missing out) and FUD (fear, uncertainty, and doubt) are common emotional triggers that can lead to poor trading decisions.

- By learning how to control your emotions and avoid FOMO and FUD, you can become a more disciplined and effective cryptocurrency trader.

Learning from your mistakes and constantly improving your skills:

- Learning from your mistakes is an important part of success in cryptocurrency trading.

- By reviewing your trading history, analysing your mistakes, and identifying areas for improvement, you can become a more skilled and knowledgeable trader.

- It's also important to continue learning and staying up-to-date with the latest trends and developments in the cryptocurrency industry.

By following these tips for success in cryptocurrency trading, you can increase your chances of success and become a more effective trader in this exciting and rapidly evolving field.

CHAPTER 8:
RISKS AND CHALLENGES OF CRYPTO TRADING

Volatility and unpredictability of cryptocurrency prices:

- Cryptocurrencies are known for their volatility and unpredictability, which can lead to significant gains or losses.

- It's important to understand the risks involved in cryptocurrency trading and to carefully manage your risk and exposure.

Hacking and security risks of cryptocurrency exchanges:

- Some Cryptocurrency exchanges have been targeted by hackers, and there have been several high-profile security breaches in the past.

- Make sure to choose a reputable and secure cryptocurrency exchange and to take steps to protect your cryptocurrency and personal information.

Regulatory risks and uncertainty:

- The regulatory environment for cryptocurrencies is constantly evolving, and there is a high degree of uncertainty and ambiguity around the legal status of cryptocurrencies in different jurisdictions.

- Stay up-to-date with the latest regulatory developments and to understand the potential impact on your trading activities.

Scams and fraud in the cryptocurrency industry:

- The cryptocurrency industry is also known for its scams and frauds, such as fake ICOs, Ponzi schemes, and phishing scams.

- Be vigilant and to carefully research any cryptocurrency projects or investment opportunities before investing your money.

By understanding the risks and challenges of cryptocurrency trading, you can make informed decisions and take steps to protect your investments and minimize your risk in this exciting and rapidly evolving field.

CHAPTER 9:
CONCLUSION AND NEXT STEPS

Congratulations! You have now completed "The Basic Guide to Crypto Trading," a comprehensive introduction to the world of cryptocurrency trading. We hope that this book has provided you with a solid foundation for becoming a more informed and effective cryptocurrency trader and investor.

In this book, we covered various topics related to cryptocurrency trading, including an introduction to cryptocurrency and blockchain technology, getting started with crypto trading, technical and fundamental analysis for trading, risk management, advanced trading strategies, tips for success in crypto trading, and the risks and challenges of crypto trading. By understanding these key topics, you should now have the knowledge and skills necessary to start your journey as a cryptocurrency trader.

However, it's important to remember that cryptocurrency trading is a rapidly evolving and complex field, and there is always more to learn. We encourage you to continue learning and growing as a trader, and to stay up-to-date with the latest trends and developments in the industry.

To further your learning, we suggest that you explore additional resources and materials related to cryptocurrency trading. Some possible next steps include:

- Following reputable news sources and blogs that cover cryptocurrency and blockchain technology.
- Joining online communities or forums for cryptocurrency traders and investors, such as Reddit or Telegram groups.
- Attending webinars or conferences on cryptocurrency trading.
- Practicing your trading skills with a demo account before risking real money.

Ultimately, the key to success in cryptocurrency trading is discipline, patience, and a willingness to learn and adapt. By applying the knowledge and skills you have gained from this book, and by continuing to learn and grow as a trader, you can become a more informed, confident, and successful cryptocurrency trader and investor.

Thank you for reading "The Basic Guide to Crypto Trading." We hope that it has been a valuable resource for you, and we wish you the best of luck on your journey as a cryptocurrency trader!

NOTES:

ABOUT THE AUTHOR

As someone who has been investing and trading cryptocurrencies for several years, I know first-hand how confusing and overwhelming it can be to navigate the complex and ever-changing world of cryptocurrency trading. I have seen people make common mistakes and lose money due to a lack of knowledge or experience in this field. This is why I decided to write this book, to help and provide them with a comprehensive and easy-to-understand guide to cryptocurrency trading. The Basic Guide To Crypto Trading book is the product of years of research and hands-on experience, and I hope that it can provide readers with the knowledge, skills, and confidence they need to become successful cryptocurrency traders and investors.

Printed in Great Britain
by Amazon

45359573R00020